POETIC LICENSE

Reaching Out for the Courage to
Speak My Truth

MAX ROYTENBERG

iUniverse, Inc.
Bloomington

Poetic License
Reaching Out for the Courage to Speak My Truth

iUniverse books may be ordered through booksellers or by contacting:

iUniverse
1663 Liberty Drive
Bloomington, IN 47403
www.iuniverse.com
1-800-Authors (1-800-288-4677)

Because of the dynamic nature of the Internet, any web addresses or links contained in this book may have changed since publication and may no longer be valid. The views expressed in this work are solely those of the author and do not necessarily reflect the views of the publisher, and the publisher hereby disclaims any responsibility for them.

Any people depicted in stock imagery provided by Thinkstock are models, and such images are being used for illustrative purposes only.

Certain stock imagery © Thinkstock.

ISBN: 978-1-4759-2806-8 (sc)
ISBN: 978-1-4759-2807-5 (hc)
ISBN: 978-1-4759-2808-2 (e)

Library of Congress Control Number: 2012909041

Printed in the United States of America

iUniverse rev. date: 11/01/2012

PREFACE

The writer is in his eighth decade. He has been
writing poetry since he found a book of
Shakespeare's poems and plays abandoned in a
junkyard at the age of twelve. The rigors of the
living experience, aside from a brief period before
marriage, at university, prevented any wholesale
output. By training, an economist, he has been a
civil servant, a food marketer, a management
consultant in Canada and in less-developed
countries, a public affairs representative for the
Canadian supermarket industry and an individual
entrepreneur. In his seventies, married at last to his
childhood sweetheart of similar age, he felt
liberated enough to free the poetry so long
suppressed within.

The material content of these pages ranges through
many of the challenges we face as inhabitants of
the western world in this twenty-first century.
The writer shares his fears and aspirations. He
appeals to his fellows to consider the futures we
are facing and will face-those our children will
face. He searches out aspects of our living that he
believes call for closer attention. He claims the
freedom to publicly explore his ideas, though they
may not, for some, be politically correct, and to
challenge his fellows to respond with attention and

action. He believes the futures we face are much less than attractive. He believes that urgent action is required to improve our prospects. He seeks to call the world to account for many things he sees that demand redress.

His protest at more orthodox ways of thinking may shock. His truth may appear far removed from conventional ways of thinking of many. He demands license to express his view of the truth. He asks some uncomfortable questions about the nature of our society, he raises issues that are difficult, even painful. They may be issues many of us may not wish to confront. He takes positions that spring from where he stands and does not apologize for that.

These poems explore the nature of a poet's work; he experiments with different forms of expression and the different ways that the poet can communicate his ideas. He advances forms that might be considered strange, bizarre, even out-of-place, exercising the license to stray beyond the edge of the accepted. Nevertheless, he seeks to entertain as well as stimulate thought. He asks questions about his role in this world, his responsibility and the responsibility of others. He tells stories. His stories ask questions. He asks the reader to go down the road a way with him and consider some of the larger questions of life in this world. If not in this place, where? He insists on the poetic license to share his thoughts and to raise these questions. **ED.**

ACKNOWLEDGEMENTS

I would like to acknowledge the role my wife, Miryom, has played in permitting me to construct the new life that made these writings possible. My Muse, Miryom has given me permission to be the selfish artist that the devotion required to produce these writings demanded. Her appreciation and enthusiasm for the messages I had to share encouraged me to persist. I thank her for believing I had something worthwhile to share.

I would like to acknowledge the contributions of all my children, David, Deborah, Judi, and Daniel. They, with their partners and the grandchildren they have blessed me with, have instructed me as to the true and primary rewards of our presence in this current existence.

I acknowledge my undying gratitude to the Life-force that governs everything we are and blessed me the gift of my life partner, lost and found again, to yield a life renewed. I acknowledgment all those unnamed souls who have provided the grist for my egotistical mill, the raw material of these offering

and thank those whose physical work enabled me
to bring this book to the public arena.
**Max Roytenberg, Pouligny-Montrachet, France,
May, 2012**

DEDICATION

This work is dedicated to Miryom, who, in spite of over fifty years of distracted inattention, had constant love on offer when I came calling, at last bold and brave enough to assault the proud tower. She has liberated me, gifting me with the power and the strength to pen these offerings.
She is the sweet "Cookie" of the High Tea of my life.
MMR, May, 2012

CONTENTS

CONTENTS-POETRY

I

What's It All About

II

What about Me?

III

Tell Me You're Story

IV

My Take on This

V

The Latest News

POETIC LICENSE

Reaching Out For The Courage To Speak My Truth

MAX ROYTENBERG

I

<u>What's it All About?</u>

Poetic License

Words run from my fingertips
like saliva from my mouth,
drawn by the remembered taste
of my living past.

The waves of memory roll over
reaches they have reached before,
bringing the minutiae,
some small rivulets of memory,
recognized but forgotten,
unappreciated,
deserving this instant's rapt attention.

I take poetic license
to recreate my past,
to cogitate, to renovate, to embellish-
and yes-to excoriate
those responsible for the evils that I see.

Perhaps this new reality is the truth.

Recitation of My Poetry

I am asked to recite of my poetry.
No bumpkin's blush be-paints my cheek,
O! Travesty of modesty-
i rather search for hearers-seek
for those listeners to my artistry
who rapt of eye, with taste sublime,
proclaim "consummate mastery"
at my control of rhythm, rhyme,
deep thought and pleasant harmony.

There might be those who raucous me condemn-
with tight-lipped glance, my pretty wit declined-
who, if but saw my cheeks incarnadined,
would praise me highly and to all exclaim,
"now lookee here! The fellow is quite awed,
so grateful he!" Though i do not gape for fame,
i play not for encouragement or prod.
I must needs bow to popular acclaim.

Ode To Eyes

This is kind of an ode to eyes,
pigs' eyes or pie size,
any old kind of eye size-
or color-if for me they "dies",
if i am their prize
and they "cries," all other guys they despise,
seeing me the object of their enterprise.

This is to the limpid gaze
if, in their poems of Junes and Mays,
i am the reason for their daze,
sitting days and days finding words
that do me praise,
and on a pedestal do me raise,
with such devotion my tiny faults could never faze,
something you could almost call a craze.
O! Happy days!

This is a poem to eyes that roam
that seek and seek-all places comb
for sight of me-there at home
they'll only be-losing all aplomb-
full of expectancy at the thrill of me-
eyes shining in the gloam-
bells ringing in the dome-

for them i write this poem.

If, as i dream, they for me roam,
with sonnets for me to fill a tome,
there is no need the crowds to comb.
I'll be waiting patiently at home.

Funny You Should Say That!

I love the silly things we say
to pass the time of day.
"Oh! Jesus!" We do say, not pray.
Oops! What was it that we meant to say?
"Hey! We dearly wish you'd really stay!"
We burn inside to say-please fly away!
We put our sweetest smiles on display-
resplendent-our true feelings to not betray.

What makes us hide our feelings so?
We act politely for social flow,
a thin veneer, so as not to show
the feelings that we hide below,
so we, in turn, won't feel the blow,
when we are the "non grata" person at the show.
We don't really believe it could ever thus be so
seeing we are the proudest cock that ever did crow.

We say "this dish is the best ever serv-ed me",
 no matter how plain it and insipid be.
"How nice this room, design-ed artistry"-
the colors and furnishings are sheer entropy.
"Your child is amazing, how well-behav-ed is he."
Spoiled rotten, best left tied and muzzled to a tree.
"Your garden shows you are a dedicated devotee."

We see bedraggled wisps of long-abandoned
forestry.

There is a devil in me that feeds on random
mockery.
The trick remains in how we deftly carry on our
spree.
The victim must forever totally unknowing be,
feeding him, benighted, with illusions through
which we'd rather he not see.
He himself is led by self-deception which is his
protective canopy,
hiding from his consciousness his own soul's
fragility
that dares not, whatever the price, see things the
way they really be,
confronting in fact the frightening rigors of life's
reality.

These Three

Wring me through the wringers of this existence
'til I am a shell,
sans love, sans hate, sans all of life.
We are ground through the masses of men, knees
in the dust,
buffeted by blows 'til from this "mortal coil" we
"shuffle off", "poor players"*.

Was a flower to grow for every tear that's shed,
this world would be an Eden.
We are spiny balls of grief
wrapped tightly in a husk shaped like a man.

We are slivers of pain, clothed human.
We are amoebae, pseudopodia cast off in all
directions,
searching for kindred souls to save us from
ourselves.

I am the ceaseless clash of molecules.
Refine my soul until my joined parts have come
apart.
See my pure elements.
See pain, loneliness and the tortures of impending
death-

the greatest of these is loneliness.

*quotes are from <u>Hamlet</u>-William Shakespeare

My Rhyme

I spin my words and make a rhyme,
'tis a very simple task-
but how to imbue the words i choose
with meaning. To simply bask
in the elegance of a verse
is something i will constantly refuse-
with messages in poetry terse
the poet makes of time much better use.

I can tell a tale without a rhyme,
images glimpsed through shadows,
wraiths weaving in and out of restive sleep,
ghosts haunting our night hours,
hidden fears that stalk our consciousness,
fully masked from ourselves.
The absent rhyme makes sharper
the pain of daily breath.

We gather comfort from our rhyming time.

Dew Drop.

A drop of dew trembles in the light,
clinging to the branch of life, hesitating
before the inevitable plunge
into hard reality.

We stand on the threshold of each living instant-
mesmerized by the effervescent stream
of life before us.
We gaze sightless into our futures.

Take pleasure in the ecstasy,
the taste, the smell, the feel
of each fleeting instant
filling our lives, amazingly,
with the potentiality for JOY.

Shall We Have A Book Launch?

Words and more words spin in my head,
spiraling to no conclusion.
Fingers claw at the keyboard,
groping for meaning. We crave results-
we are in the business of results-
some rational reason for our being,
not an enema of the mind
to be wasted on the empty pages
littering our onrushing dawns.

I digest the mind's meanderings
for that nugget of truth,
rescuing treasure from the dross-so much dross-
perhaps worthy of being an embellishment
on the digested fibers of the magnificent trees
that graced our lost horizons-
that graced our inherited empty spaces.
Do i offer only mental sewage prettified
with fastidious pretension?
Shall this work be worthy of our sacrifices?

Shall we have a book launch?

Sea Sing Song

Today i am at sea.
Leaden waters shimmer
past the shoulders of the leviathan i am astride,
casting a million billion photons into my eyes,
forming images in my brain.

The highlights rival the sparkles of the night sky.
We rush forward
as into the darkness of a womb
that will give birth come morning
to another expanse of ocean
or a welcoming port.

I am overcome by the vastness
of the blinded face of darkness.
I feel like an insect on a petrified sliver
of life afloat on a rushing tide.
Water, water everywhere,
below and seemingly above
in the endless sky.

On this craft we are another wandering speck,
existing in our own private universe.
We carry on with no thought

to our insignificance in the vastness
that surrounds us.
We are full of ourselves-so busy-
a teeming ant-hill afloat,
the sole manned planet spinning around the sun
we greet eagerly each morning.
We consume with abandon
countless mounds of food.
We are crowds
of humans seeking eagerly for diversions
on our many-tiered raft in this endless ocean.

I am not proud of the song I am singing.

Can i imagine some useful purpose
for my being here?
Can i provoke a sonata
that will stir a heart, rouse a spirit,
stimulate a new vision,
so entrance my kind that I will tempt one
to engage in a new beginning
making my sibilant song significant?
Or, will these just be sad singsong syllables
sinking into the sound of the sea?

Better Crushed Petal Cold

Crush the petal, waiting, willing, wanting,
burning, consuming agony – dying
to enclose one instant's raging sweetness.

Changing color in the sun, briefly,
brown and withered, without scent,
blazing cruel flame-cold.

Better that way.
Buddha's crushed petal
without scent, snow cold – loveless.

Better changeless eastern snows,
faint blue cones in the distance.
Better Buddha's withered woman,
Himalayan wilderness, detached,
no sun; no hurry; cold.
Better.

Flying Away

We spend a lot of our time burrowing away
into the new places we are in
so we can feel more comfortable
where we are strangers.

Talk to a neighbor, show some interest,
glimpse their lives, share some personal detail,
buy a plant, mount a curtain,
attend a community scene.
Suddenly it is more comfortable-
people greet you by name-
you've arrived at your place.

When you go away people ask
when you are coming back?
You have become imprinted on their lives
in ways that make your presence
important to them. They are jealous
of the time you spend away.
You have become part
of their extended family circle.

When i fly away now i know
that it is, in some ways, an act of betrayal.
Though unspoken, my new friends

feel a secret hurt. I see it in their eyes.

I am tearing at the fabric of their lives.
They don't think of that when they do it to us,
but they feel it when we do it to them.

When we re-unite at that future time,
we have some repairing to do.
We have composed something
valuable to the people around us.

I realize that i am sometimes resentful
when friends i value go away,
denying me the pleasure of their presence.
I ache for their piece of my life being there
when i reach out for its essence.

Do others feel the way i do?
I know we take it for granted that
those feelings are there
when we think of family, siblings,
children and others we are close to
in living our family lives.

The ultimate betrayal comes
when the people we value die.
We are shocked, stunned.
We have lost the access we had counted on.
We are sometimes angry.

We must console ourselves with memories,
one-way conversations.
They fly away and leave us.
They leave without asking for our permission.

Sometimes when i leave
i feel a secret satisfaction-
Take that for not appreciating me
as you should have!

Do the dead who have retreated
to their secret place feel that?

Lost In Thought

The miracle of being. the spark of life,
phantom thoughts, fleeting,
the incessant internal strife.

When do these thoughts begin to exist?

The electric thought sought,
just electrons in the mist,
'til clearly vocalized, impinged,
transmitted to another's brain,
or printed, organized on paper,
on a computer, or verily in stain?

Was it lost in the corridors of time,
wisdom potentially advancing humankind,
cruelly tossed, interred,
buried with its human slime?

Listen! There is quiet breathing.
See! That person sitting there!
Mayhap there a mind is seething,
in that body,
in that chair,
knowing the questions we should pose,
knowing the most important task to perform by far-

or,
if that is a jewel we already chose,
answer what is the future of our star.

Leave us space to ruminate
we all need space to breathe,
but fail not then to communicate
the real treasure hiding underneath.

II

<u>What About Me?</u>

Existential Rewards

The words run from my mouth and through my
fingers, slim evidence of the crowded mass,
conflicting-conflicted-telling the slippery truth of
who i am.

Will the evidence traced on the pages of words i
leave behind capture what i am, what i was, what i
am becoming, truer, more truly, than the bare facts
of my live-ed life?

Are our words lies, sheer imaginings, fed by the
inflated egos we inhabit, shining up the wreckage
of our failures, our weaknesses, our sayings and
not doings, shadings, shading with half-truths,
what we/i , felt we/i, could have- should have-done
better?

I glory in my survival against all odds, self-
destructive behaviors, foolishness, carelessness,
stupid bull-headedness, leaving fate to chance,
willful blindness to consequences, at risk to me and
those around me so dependent on my good
judgment for sustenance-how is that to my credit?
Where was the obligation to care, consider, ponder,

examine the needs-awareness of the needs of those in my trust.

Why the blind focus on the satisfaction of my own needs-my sole focus on feeding those needs-that need to gain with my own hands-brain-will-the fickle, insubstantial, sometimes unworthy prizes at the heart of my aspirations, often turning to dust in my mouth as i achieved their taste?

How is it i have earned the love of my nearest and dearest when what i have done is so insufficient to merit this award? How did i deserve this precious-my existential reward?

Am i telling your story as well?

Spectral Thoughts

I   SEND

MY

THOUGHTS

ACROSS

THE

SPATIAL

SPECTRUM

THAT

LEADS

TO

A

CONCLUSION.

CAN

YOU

FOLLOW

MY

THOUGHTS

TO

THE

END.

Incandescent

The light that flows from youth casts a glow that lights our way. I am transfixed! Stunned! Beauty incandescent! The strength of their life-force seizes me by the throat so i am breathless.

See the brightness! See all the possibilities. A pantheon is arrayed before us that pales for me the poor residues i leave behind. Let me rest a moment with the view of God's firmament before my eyes-the incandescent glow of youth.

Rhapsody

Hands together clapping to the rhythm of our
yearning souls
engaged in ceaseless searching
for their perfect mates,
making the world's lonely two's into ones,
lonely halves into wholes.

Mysterious tendrils and celestial winds,
perhaps changing fates,
perhaps yours and mine,
dictate finding my You,
destined, long before your even being,
my completion, waiting for me,
long before my even seeing.
Together, we are a rhapsody.

Le Mot Juste*

Astir, astride, stirring, striated, strand. mythic, mythical, rhythmic, arthritic, arresting. How satisfying and fulfilling if the word's just right for the situation!

The time, the place, if i am just right for the time and place, if i am just right for the situation, do i make the time and place just right? If i were not there would another step up-and be just right for the situation? Would another word do just as well? Would another man do just as well?

Or will all be lost for the want of a nail, "le mot juste*"? Our kingdom for want of the "mot juste*"? Our world, for "l'homme juste*"? Right now we really need "l'homme juste*" with "le mot juste*". Where is he?

* a French term meaning just the right word and the right man for the situation

The Secrets

The steady gaze that mine meets, no sighs,
i see there secrets in the eyes,
calm and cool and seeming wise,
a mask perhaps hiding hidden cries.

Like a drowning man sinking in that pool
my thoughts go breathless into that cool,
seize fierce my will, don't play the fool!
Learn slowly the lessons in that school!

Imaginary phantasms screech and cry and reel,
scars cut deep, fleshy parts still feel,
images pour forth from fissures without a seal.
eyes blink with pain from wounds that never heal.

I kissed a cheek; it seared my skin with sudden
flush,
i wondered at secrets firing that cheek to sudden
blush,
what thoughts roused blood in Beauty's mind to
rush?
My heart it bounded, the world in a sudden hush.

I gaze at eyes so seeming wise,
they tell no lies, tell they no lies?

I rage at histories, ideas, i despise,
i feel pain at the secrets hidden in those eyes.

The steady gaze that meets my eye, no sighs,
i see there secrets in those eyes,
calm and cool and seeming wise,
a mask mayhap hiding hidden cries.

Sounds And Noise

A paradox that both equate, noise makes sounds
and sounds make noise.
But, sounds that elevate the heart and mind are not
just noise,
noise that deafens and strains the cochlear antennae
to the edge of pain and beyond.

The screams of the injured and the dying,
the weeping and the wailing of the lost
who have lost everything,
who make us retch and turn away,
covering our eyes to the pain and horror,
cringing and hiding from Death
that comes like thunder in War and Peace.

These are not just sounds,
but noises that punish the yet living.
If i hear the sound of a child's laugh,
all trebles and tinkles,
a lover's whisper in a loved one's ear,
wise counsel from a graying head-
all are dreams of life renewed.

A soliloquy by Shakespeare,
sparkling with allusions and illusions,

spirals our minds into the infinite,
into new worlds in microcosm.
Beethoven and Mozart, Gershwin and Bob Dylan,
Miles Davis and Joni Mitchell-
the Moldau, the Bolero by Ravel,
the New World Symphony-
how many there are!

All these sounds are not just noise,
but really our souls reaching out of sight.

Fish Story

Tell a tale of fishery
and ancient forms of life.
It seems that all forms of life
of a common source were bred.
The dinosaur, it came from ancient bird life rife,
while man, tortuously, from the first amphibian
fish was led.

The tale, they say, from common genes in life was
traced,
their magic worked on hand and foot, man's
wonder, the opposed thumb,
making all the difference in the challenging world
we faced,
with less bone-bound brains, making us, compared
to chimps, less dumb.

Combinations of genes, A, C, G, T, timing and
intensity in our schemes,
life essences dazzle us being much alike in every
living thing,
and yet for all our sameness, presents such very
different scenes-
incredibly, tiny changes worlds of difference bring.

The wonder is that so much depends on how
simple things interact,
how in the cut and thrust of living stress, where so
much can go wrong,
so many living things arrive with the needed
combinations still intact,
making us wonder if we do damage rescuing
human errors in our throng.

That's our tale; the complex is so simple-now do
you really see?
A jigsaw fishy puzzle is at the root of every
person's family tree.

Breathing to Death

Living, as in a one-celled diatom,
or better, pseudopodia, arms and legs worming off
in all directions.

Each extremity making human contact intertwines,
affecting us deeply- not-so-deeply-tangentially.

We are altered, unalterably, inextricably,
there is incised evidence of our passing
on the lives we touch.

Existentially, a random-not so random- life-force.
in the medium we inhabit. impacts our lives and
the lives of those around us.

Driven by our emotions, sometimes hidden even
from ourselves,
harnessed, or rogue, for good or evil, incipient,
for harmony or scorched earth scourge.
We affect life wherever our extremities reach.
Willy-nilly, we consume ourselves and those
around us with every breath we take.
Over our time, every one of us, with every breath
we take, is breathing to death,

It is not too late! Look back!
We are imperfect with the best of will.
We are weak even when we are sometimes strong.
We are often weak servants of our baser impulses.

Breathe in and out and then look back.
Are your paths marked by monuments to Life or
Death?

Do I Repeat Myself?

Do I repeat myself? Are my words mere mania?
Monomania? Or emphasis on an an important
point-points?

I cast my eyes the world around. I see threats on
every horizon.
Am i wrong to raise the alarm as true prophets did
of old, reluctant and fearful of their burden?

I glory in my little life, pleasure in the sweet
moments-a loved one's touch and caring act. Is this
mere "pussycats and flowers" excreted from a
maundering mind?

Does the price of preaching dictate surrender of
these joys?

I see my children flourish and being planted firm. I
glory in the new life surrounding me with the
potential for new starts and new horizons- am i
unwise to peek, transfixed with wonder, around the
infinite curve of time?

I talk of my people, a living relic, living and dying
in the same breath. They so impact the world, men

cannot tolerate the Beauty of their being, seeing themselves smaller in their own sad eyes.

I search into the secrets of being, the wonder of the human form, the beauty of a flower, the mystery of the atom, the unknowable spark of life, the secret space where God resides.

In what form shall our world persist?
I wonder why i survive to tell my story.

Must i tell it?

Why was i chosen to live my so fortunate life, billions around the world eking out their time on the miserable edge of existence?

I do what i do. Must i surrender my quiet life?
Why can't i still my voice? Why must i shout?

I am in the grip of inner forces that will out or i explode. Constellations align me for my ultimate cosmic journey.

But, i repeat myself!

Poetry

Poets have throughout time
chiseling on their little rhyme,
grandly, small thoughts displayed,
with their audiences' emotions played
to suit their fancies-this is their crime.
The worlds within their minds
like jeweled creative finds
cast reflections, see them crawl
like living images, their own lives but rinds,
holding our worlds in thrall.
There is magic here to see for all.

There are frozen lives poets can set free,
those carrying congealed messages inside,
hidden things we often hide, we see
that their gentle touches for us expose
the festering things that cruelly indispose.

Poetry sometimes cleanses us, cleans
up the fetid thinking, strife
offering paths to a better life.
Treasure, then, our poets, every bard,
we need them with us, life is hard-
they can reward us, welcome solace give
and teach us somehow how to better live,
describing for us ways and even means.

There's A Lady They Call The Gypsy

What dreams we have of life and where will they
take us?

Some of us never go far from where we were
spawned, imagining, always, we would see those
faraway places.

Today it's so easy to find something on the
internet, cheap, too, and away you go.
But many of us just wait for something to happen,
or some person to happen-and it doesn't. We settle
for what we have at hand.

Television and the internet bring us the world,
programs fantastical and experiences we would
never have-
or see it on YouTube, the past, the present and the
future.

That's something, but not enough for those
who willingly expose themselves to the
humiliation of publicly showing their weaknesses
and stupidities to a national audience, totally
without sense of self-
just so they can have the experience.

"Look, Ma, I'm on the net, on television. I'm famous!"

This is the high point of their lives
in their search for that one spark of self esteem in
accord with their distorted view of the world,
totally insensitive to their caricature of life.

No need now to visit the gypsy fortune teller.

Fire In The Hole!

Fire in the hole! Fire in the hole!
The traditional cry of a bygone age, explosive set
to play an accustomed role.
In my mind I liken it to ideas- gauge the fire it
lights in a special man's soul.
Address the concept of God to feed man's fear of
doing wrong and paying the awful toll,
Jeremiah and Ezekiel described it-foreswear
transgression or you lose your world-the whole.

The power of ideas can shape men's lives, can
change our world-its form complete-entire,
numbers count little when a burning thought
contrives to move the masses- among them lighting
a burning fire
raging through their minds, an idea that even
survives
brute force that's threatened when it does belief
inspire,
even in violence's face, the faithful it drives.
This is a human need-we do it require,
imbibed with mother's milk-inspiration in human
hives-

motivates a man to seek the path that for him is
right.
Will yours be the idea that will light a fire in a
mind?
Will the picture that you paint set a blessed wind in
flight?

Will you be caught up by a great wave of
humankind searching, ever searching, to turn
darkness into light?

Many are our dark places that we can on earth here
find crying out to us! Come! Make this dark place
bright!

To see them not, we must surely be willfully blind

if we bend not common will to make the wrong
things right.

 Light it, light a fire in the hole! See the light!

To you, and you, the human role-be brave! To you
it is now assigned!

Words Fail Me

Trickling electronics bleed through the neurons of
my brain, pulsating charges culminating, through
the conservation of energy, in verbal emanations,
written demonstrations, emotions surging to show
evidence of life. I suck up the stimuli, engorging
my senses, willy-nilly, sensate; i am the living
vessel into which all this is poured.

I am, all of me, on the receiving end.
A grey raincloud shreds against the blue envelope
in which we are enfolded. I see a solitary path,
high-hedged, a burbling stream through sunny
banks, springtime-enriched blooms yearn for small
children to pick them-a child obliges with
innocence and look of trust-who would reprove
God's cherub?
The child basks in the unconscious assumption of
love as if caressed by the sunny brush of a
butterfly's wing.
Feel the precious weight of a child's body leaning,
this being accepting you within the ambit of its
life.
Glory in the sensation and hold your tongue! A
harsh word would be corrosive,
long working its poison over a lifetime-
speak gently when you do-with a loving touch.

Wise counsel can turn your word into a legacy for life for the subject. Patient enquiry and response yields the golden dividends of trust and consultation through all your hoped-for futures. You stand on the cusp of creating the unseen you desire.

Love found, love squandered, accidents of fate and misadventure, the catastrophes that haunt the lonely, the silent yearnings of desolated lives. Pain and regret stalk the unmade existences. What will be your role in the shape of the lives you touch?

Fortunate unions of hearts and minds, bodies and common needs-lives are illuminated by the bright light of warmth in hearts that a loving relationship can create. You can set in place a spark that with time will be a steady flame enhancing the whole of a life.

I have seen the stark contrast of a quiet peace or the acid pain of cravings, souls misaligned, leading good people to a tortured fabric of living that is a curse. I have seen the wounds and scars that indelibly mark their living's rhyme. Can you see what your choices of action yield through the mists of time?

See a table festooned with wholesome foods, gathered and prepared by loving hands, relish the taste of heart's desire on your tongue and in your heart and mind. Was there ever such a feast? Will you not swallow the bile and speak sweetly?

Feel the anguish of dashed hopes-decrying pasts, shredding presents and futures. Lives are as delicate as a spider's web, sparkling with the jeweled beads of our emotions. Can you not perceive the awful power that lies at your command?

Shall i describe human dreams of the infinite cosmos, the unimaginable that we strive to imagine, the Maker we strive to believe in, the one we seek in faith? How can He remake our lives? How can you remake your life and the lives of those around you with the power given into your hands?

Where is the genius of those who came before me to help me describe the power we have to forge our own indescribable existence in our own image? Words fail me.

Apple Pie

We have to be serious about important things!
The world is warming and the polar cap may melt,
the clash of civilizations may bring one hundred
years of war; pollution in our water may
emasculate our men. Will the plenty of today erase
tomorrow from our ken?

What fevers more my brow as round the world i
turn searching streets without surcease, every nook
and every cranny
where human's hearts' do beat, be it humble, or so
stern, simple hut, or promenade, on hill or dale-I
am that canny,
there be here some eating place, there must be one
I bet,
do they have it on the menu, some apple pie that I
can "et"?

So sad, how often they appear; the words are
printed there,
some version of reality, thoughtlessly thrown upon
a plate.
No love, no care, no charity, a travesty of soul-
beware!

How dare they so presume and to us offer up this
fate,
ignoring aspirations, pure, of divine excellence we
share.

But rarely, O! Too rarely! We, suddenly strike the
mother lode!
Crust that's short and crumbly, apple, firm and tart,
a flowing juiciness from the heart of fruit, here the
secret code,
the mystery we can't define, present in every part,
sugar, lemon, cinnamon, all well and truly fired,
creating, for the fortunate, taste's symphony, full
attired.

We all have our priorities, as lives we singly lead,
to find the things, important, use well the time, we
heed.
I've built here my monuments, brought children
for my breed,
lessons i have taught them, the same to all my
seed.
Talked much, perhaps too often, of tasks that lie
ahead,
my mission, now transmuted, apple pie becomes
my bread.

Strangers In An Irish Pub

I came here from a different place
and from a different time. Where i grew up they
called it the beer parlor, not a place for nice people,
not a nice place, with nasty smells and, often,
fights that spilled out into the street. Nice ladies
didn't go there. It wasn't chic like a Bar could be,
all dressed up with shiny clothes and fancy décor.

Things are much different here in Ireland today.
I can imagine in the past that coming home from
work it would have been natural to stop at the Pub
for a pint and a warm meal. Home would be cold
and overrun with kids.

A fella' would need a pint or two before going
home to face the wife, trapped there all day with
little ones, the cooking and cleaning, trying to keep
the place livable, with only a peat fire, if that, when
the money was short. Maybe sometimes the wife
would have to come to the Pub to drag her man
home before all the food money was gone.

Maybe that's not true and i am imagining the
worst, being a stranger and not knowing the life
here in Ireland. I know that sometimes happened
where i grew up.

Here they tell me that drinking is a really serious matter, not to be taken lightly and not to be abandoned while one can still stand.

Last week i went into a Galway Pub for one of the best experiences of my life. It was crowded and i had to push in. I found my own little nook, pressed against the musical back of one of a group of seven musicians crowded into a corner.

One man played a large cardboard box with a long mop handle and a rope leading into the middle of the box. He had tape around his fingers to protect them as he strummed on the rope to produce a booming sound.

Another man played an Irish bagpipe. There was one woman with a guitar, diminutive, pretty, of young middle-age and modest dress. She was a songstress.

Two others had guitars, one who acted as the leader, the other, a great bear of a man, danced in his place while he played and sang. There was one man who played the banjo and another who played the flute.

All sang when their mouths weren't otherwise occupied, harmonizing with the momentary prophet expounding on the sermon. Each offering was an improvisational masterpiece, the leader taking the group on flights of song and verbal variations that appealed to his or her inclination.

The publican stoked the music with a continuing stream of liquids, refilling empty vessels that appeared. The pleasure of the musicians in the creations they were offering was patent in their smiling faces and dancing eyes. The people crowded into the Pub danced in their places, roaring out the words of the songs they knew, clapping and shouting.

For a few moments the fortunate onlookers were joined in a unique happening, strangers becoming like one, united in their common enjoyment, sharing glances and smiles of pleasure. We were strangers but intimate in the unity of the experience that bound us together.

The set ended, the musicians dispersed, participants returned to their brews or drifted off, abandoning intimacy.

We were strangers once again.

Bloody Nerve

Just because we think we can spin a rhyme or tell a
tale, just because we live in America
and the world is our oyster. Just because we've
grown up thinking we can say anything we want to
about anything we want to, we say outrageous
things about things we know very little about.

Sometimes we have perceptive insights that open
people's minds to ideas they would never have
arrived at. In the hope of the latter we have the
bloody nerve to do the former.

The things we say or write about sometimes hurt,
we have the bloody nerve to accept that as
collateral damage for the good work we think we
do.

We are the bloody nerve of the body politic,
the canary in the mine, the early detection system
that few listen to until it is too late.

Are we getting on your nerves?

III

<u>Tell Me Your Story!</u>

Happenstance!

It was just a moment of inattention.
We were crowding at the barrier,
pushing and shoving.
Those making it through would live for a while,
those not, might die-how did we know-would die.
Those most fearful, more knowing, were already
ignoring the niceties of civilized behavior
drummed into us as children, climbing, clambering
over the bodies of those standing in their way.

In an instant there was a melee.
My identity card slipped from my sweaty fingers.
Bending down to recapture the precious scrap of
pasteboard, i was knocked down, climbed over,
kicked away as an impediment! Lost to sight!
Where is it? Nowhere to be seen!

Has someone, keen-eyed, seen a precious jewel
and snapped it up? The crowd rushes on as we mill
about, an eddy in the river. I scrabble about
hopelessly. The crowd continues to stream through
the barrier, a barrier we cannot pass through
without our precious scrap of cardboard. We are
going nowhere, we are nobody in a no-mans' land.

We remain in malevolent hands with no proof of who we are. We are alive, but we are no-one, our deaths are just a detail. We are like millions in the past. We are like millions in the present.

Are we to be like millions in the future?

Which happenstance world shall we choose?

The Poet's Secret

Do you know what it is?
What is it the poet has to say?
Has he conceived a secret message?
no-one has ever brought to sight?
Or is it the beauty of the language,
the confections he conjures up,
the ebb and flow of rhymes so soothing
we long to inhale them again and again
for the hit, the trip, the trances.

Visions of beauty or horror
in arresting language that shiver loose
shadowy phantasms in our cowering
 minds, connect our conscious with
our subconscious, indelibly imprinting
this instant there forever.

The poet's secret is the key he finds
to unlocking the resonances in your mind,
raping you if need be, with his assault on your
beliefs to seduce you to his view That fragment
of your life when he has your attention,
he will reach out to seize your essence,
to hold you forever captive, if he can.

You did not realize when you opened
the covers of that book
that you were in danger of losing your soul,
and surrendering your mind.

Damn You!

I was just going to tell you something important
and you interrupted me.
Now, i've lost my train of thought
and it may never come back.

I know it was important,
in fact, it may have been the most important thing
i have ever had to say.
Now it's gone. It is gone forever!
I just know it!

hate it when that happens
because most of what i say
may be just a waste of time,
but this time it was really important!

Do you see the way the sun shines,
slithering through the leaves,
the light all dappled where it lands,
like freckles marking kisses on the landscape,
making it seem really friendly and inviting?
I want to roll around in the grass so that i am
one with the light, tattooed with warming spots
all over my body. I know i would feel the warmth
of the sun in spots if i took off all my clothes.

Did i tell you i slept very well last night?
It must be because we made love-
you were so loving! Breakfast yesterday was
so good too-a dream-poached eggs on toast-
just perfect! And the marmalade!
O! That marmalade-bitter and sweet-
on the buttered toast.

Did i tell you how much i love you?

Damn you for interrupting my thought!

Now it's lost forever!

My Raining Days

I am a poet. I accept it now. I am not just rubbing my tummy. There is something important in me that demands release.

I worry that my ideas, the tracks i leave on paper, the nanotechnic, neuronic impulses that can span a universe, will not reach, will not strike a responsive chord, will not spark the light of understanding in another's eyes, will not bring pleasure to another mind- your mind-as it did to mine.

I worry. Still the ideas flow from me without let, without waiting for answers to my fears. In the end I must write for myself.

It is raining on the precious few days left to me to tell my story, raining challenges to the lives we lead. My images flow on whether i apply myself or not, whatever the weather in the places where i am, whether it is welcoming or not, whether my ideas roil in the turmoil of my place or find purchase in the ordered confines-the pages-of time, my time and yours-in ways serving a purpose.

I cringe at the arrogance in me that assumes
without question that what i have to say is worth
your time of day and mine. I plunge on, heedless,
laboring, planting my seeds-hoping-hoping that
beauty will germinate, beauty will appear before
your eyes, that your mind will be fed, that nutrients
for living will flow in the darkening cloudy days i
am raining my ideas on world.

The Poet's Gift

Can you imagine the world he lives in?
He's never where you think.
He may be there and look you in your face,
but see, he does not blink
His mind is many miles away,
away on phantom moons,
perhaps even on a distant star.
inspecting ancient runes.
You cannot trust that he's aware
that you may have come from far
to speak to him, an appointment duly made.
He has departed to dig nuggets with his spade;
maybe in his mind he sees images of despair,
visions, ideas. transmuted into word display,
to conjure up worlds he can with reality array.
Be gentle-he does not seek to injure,
wound, or show you disrespect.
The blank face before you masks kaleidoscopes
the eyes do not reflect.
The poet is a special creature
who inhabits our Nows sole in part,
his mind races, riots ever, but listen,
he may yet share his inner heart,
a thought evoked changing your view of life,
or relieve a pain, an existence full of strife,

help discern a treasured beauty that you simply
failed to see,
discover, suddenly, a secret with the power to set
you free.
Alchemy and witchcraft may seem the mysteries
he wields,
but visions for your better life may be the gift it
yields.

Music In Poetry

I remember some of the best moments of my life
were spent listening to music.
All my life I dreamed of making beautiful music.
I studied the violin at the urgent demand of my
mother
who believed that every person should be trained
to make beautiful sounds.
No person's education was complete
without having acquired that skill.
Both my older sister and i spent years
trying to acquire those necessary skills,
my sister more successfully than i.
I remember grunting with the effort,
urgently commanding my fingers and hands
to reproduce the melodic singing sounds
gifted me on those pages
in the mysterious calligraphy of past genius.
All to no avail.
I had neither the physical dexterity
nor the sense of rhythm
nor the ear, nor the mind
to translate that language
into the harmonies they represented.
All i was left with was a love of music,
an appreciation that i cherish to this day.

The unexpressed arpeggios inside me
still seek companions in my ears.

My children have proved more fortunate than me.
Without urging they have taught themselves
the harmonies, the sounds that fill me with joy.
In my daydreams I produce music like George,
poetry that is my "Rhapsody in Blue",
my "American in Paris",
my "All that Jazz",
my "Scintillating Rhythm".
This is my contribution to the music of the spheres,
i hear myself grunting as of old
in my effort to sow beauty in our world that way.
Can you hear the songs i sing to you in my words?
Do my words resonate with the harmonies
i crave to pour in your ear?
Do you hear the music in my poetry?
Shall i sing louder, softer, or just be quiet?
Do i have the knack?
O George, why did you have to die so young?

Feel The Free!

Do you feel it? Think about it! Right now! Let it all go!
Feel the feeling of freedom wash over you!
Smell the roses; see the shimmering reflections of life's juices, masquerading as dew that can make your life sparkle. Get some perspective on the longer run-what really matters.

Why did i wait until i was old before i let myself let it go? I was so full of all the things i had to do-must do-right now and there was no time. I couldn't do it, wound up like a spring. What if i had been able to let go-let release wash over me and get a new perspective on my life, on my World? Would i not have done even better-been better-a master of the universe?

Why did it take me fifty years to get it, that it all doesn't really matter that much? Not as much as the smile of your bride, not as much as the laughter of your child. Hey! That's the big deal, the thing you will remember all your life-and at the end of your life.

I know everybody says that stuff, but it is really true! I remember! Easy to talk now-why couldn't i do it then, all wrapped up in my urgencies? I look back at my losses-the wouldas, shouldas and couldas.

Do better than i did while there's still time to salvage the losses.
Can you do it?
You can do it!
Lighten up and feel the free'

Island in the Ocean

Furious attacks on rock-bound coasts, unceasing,
tide-borne, wind-borne, time-borne forces grind
away at where we stand, what we stand for.

Can we stand our ground? We are islands in the
ocean of events cascading on the who we are, the
what we are, shaping us, shaping the ground we
have built with bitter experience to find a space we
can stand upon. See how ocean shores are shaped
by the forces of nature, the deluge of forces
grinding away what they were yesterday into the
spaces they fill today.

The world we see today is different from the one
we saw yesterday, or a hundred years ago. Small
wonder that the island I am, that you are, is very
different from what we stood for at a different
time.

Small wonder that I have a different view of many
things, small wonder that i grasp desperately to
find a piece of ground i can preserve against the
forces of nature, man, the flood of events
undreamed of in my former times-former
nightmares-imagined in the face of facts that now

surpass them. Today's flood of events, its waves pounding away at my island-hear the desperation in my voice, in my words- shake the ground i stand on.

Can i defend my place, stand my ground and preserve my personal island in the ocean of Life?

Looking Ahead From Behind

We know we carry with us all our baggage carefully packed from the past. No-one really starts fresh each day. Try as we might, the unconscious imprints of past happenings condition the responses we offer.

Some of it is good, our learnings guide us so we smoothly meet the expected with the expertise our conditioned knowledge permits-we do not stumble-we are experienced.

Sometimes the new challenges we face are betrayed by our conditioned responses-we need to rethink how we respond to a new situation in ways for which our past cannot provide a guide.

If we are not open to the possibility of potential new approaches, we do ourselves and our futures an injustice which leads to error.

But, how to know the difference? How to maintain alertness sufficient to perceive we face a new world demanding a new approach?

Can we look ahead from behind and clearly see the future?

Being Smart

Hear the rootin', hear the tootin', the young ones goin' on again, talkin' about the smart stuff, how the world will be all smart Then.

Looking around my living world, I am not a bit surprised all our visions of the future have been so compromised. Now analyzed, and with the passing time, fully digitized, bits and pieces, to be from time to time excised, including, as is the custom, being traditionally circumcised.

These are just beginnings, the harbingers of what's to come, we are building parallel worlds of which we know not yet the sum. For every shape of matter that in our world exists, as we turn and twist, each element does our electronic path resist, a phantom world we build as real as the one we feel and touch,

Converging matter electronified, unified in a new world, very much. In this world, building substance only our young can imagine, functioning automatically, repair or alert, only a random human in the cabin.

Using our mobile to buy our groceries, setting our electronic tea kettle on boil, setting the temperature in fridge and in the home, making foods that never spoil.

Finding answers to our questions that we never knew the How to ask. Finding cures for man's afflictions that we never dared to task, can we find the magic of bringing peace to the warring human heart? That remains for man the challenge, to be really, really smart.

Past Imperfect

The wonder of the futures we create in our mind's eye, we ride astride the horses of our wishful thinking, galloping gaily through the vistas we want to see, work to see, hope to see, air-brushed with proposed efforts, allies and emasculated enemies of our hopeful imaginings, dreaming our strivings toward our goals.

The past, with all its events leaves us yet wanting, victories and defeats, harrying us to further efforts, scarred and wounded by our failings, the acid of regret eating at our self esteem, our anger at our weaknesses feeding determination to master our destinies, concentrate our forces, refashion our past imperfect into that future world that lies yet just beyond our grasp.

Pretense And Retribution

Sing a song of pretense, a pocketful of lies,
corrodes the body politic, hear the hopeful cries.
No room here for the innocent who search for
simple truth,
our world no longer speaks to that, we answer to
the brute.

We cover up with honeyed words to mask the
shames we hide,
while the helpless and the powerless are simply
pushed aside.
The suited men we self-appoint because we relish
not their job,
they fill the air with words and sham while the
weak the strong do rob.

How often do we seek appeasement to spare
ourselves the cost
of confronting the injustices when we fear a cause
is lost?
Why should we let that trouble us? We could some
assets lose-
aside from blood and treasure-end up with a
serious bruise.

We cannot hide complicity; we know we have
some blame,
but we bluster and we obfuscate, turn our faces
from the shame.
Our history shows our time will come if injustice
faces not some defense.
Time and time again our world has shown we pay
dearly- this pretense.

Georgia: La Danse Macabre

Flows tranquil the pace of the dark cruiser, driven through the night,

sleepy, transported, cocooned, rigors, dangers, lurking in half light,

child prodigy with magic fingers, war-torn solidarity, a motive bright.

Sudden-the alarms, sharp noises, stops and starts, explosive sound,

motors roar, tires squeal, surges of fierce movement and feet that pound,

confusion, fear, unknown menace threatens the peaceful flow of thought,

high alert, guardians watchful, imparting tension-risks and fear are crowned.

The child cowers in his cage, creative urges in a pool of fear is drowned.

Command the fleet to rescue the tiny visitor, with danger fraught.

The press arrives to tell the world what the Bear's tyranny has wrought, renowned, the writer, creeps into the cage where prodigy is caught,

to record the sound and sentiment-he comes from the world away for naught.

Send a picture telling tales to the world a thousand words cannot.

The task is done, the writer exits with all the tales he came for and sought-

a shot rings out! With blood the writer's copy book now blot.

Set the scene, the convoy rushes, speeding forward as if pursuit is hot-

passing cortege, moving slowly, bearing a soldier's body who also fought-

dance on our world, another monument with blood on it to mark the spot.

In Memoriam

Like a shock from the blue, such sad news- is it
really true?
A life struck down in fullest stride, depended on,
on every side,
our messenger to the Irish young, our spokesman
to the foreign throng,
our guardian of histories past, struggling fiercely to
ensure it last.

My pain at having lost a friend,
no thought that it could ever end,
humor, wisdom, fun, deep thought,
discovered, sudden, for my lucky lot.
Discovered treasures, here, unsought,
visions, vistas, from his mind wrought.
Warmth, compassion, did to all comers send,
to all a welcome ear he did lend.

Will my weeping bring you back?
Why did you run from our life's track?
Why was the care owed you unkept?
Why were we all left here bereft?
How long before my angers fade?
We carelessly allowed your life unmade?
I rail against my God so cruel,

an unexplained loss, so harsh His rule.

We turn now to our task-to soldier on
and see his living's vision drawn
into reality, our story told,
as did we in Irish life unfold,
the role we played making life here better,
I's, crossed T's, rules followed to the letter,
in so doing sharing all our gifts,
blending cultures, repairing ancient rifts.

Hear me, now, my friends around,
his life to our credit did redound.
We must give thanks and make our peace
with "Rafael's" going, his end of lease.
Let's band together and face the task,
the challenges he left us here unmask.
with willing spirit all our efforts lend
to confront our world-repair and mend.

The Promised Land

Breathless water, overcome with eagerness, rushes
down rock-strewn hills
bearing brimming life to thirsty plants
waiting patiently in the sun, bringing flowers for
children, forget-me-nots for lovers-and bread.
Blood, sweat and tears water stony fields around
the globe.

Time and time and time again the
fertile gardens did create burning envy,
rousing greed, yielding death and destruction. We
slough off parts. We surrender parts to comfort,
parts to fear, parts to cruel steel, fire and ashes.
Remnants, life-forces flowing on, make fertile
others' potentialities.

There is the one place, promised long ago,
remembered in our minds, remembered with our
bodies, remembered with our treasure, a garden
neglected as we were driven to the far outskirts of
the circling globe, remembered as we tended
others' heritage wherever we were flung.

Abandoned gardens turned to swamp and desert,
desolate rock-bound hills and forlorn valleys
despised by all but we-always remembered,
dreamt of -that "land of milk and honey".

Here we make our stand. Here our swamps are
drained, our deserts made to bloom. Once barren
hills now shimmer and shine with the green of
growth. The ranges of our habitations explode to
decorate the barren slopes, sparkling with the
creative genius of our heritage.

 Back to back we stand withstanding the greed and
envy of what we build. Here our epic story flowers
and flourishes on once stony ground, reborn as a
garden, rebuilding a vision of the world's Eden.

Here we die if need be-live here, if blessed be-
giving new life to our Promised Land.

IV

<u>My Take On This</u>

The Sweep Of Bloody Times

I am swept away by my connectedness, my
disconnectedness, raging, I want to tear my flesh,
bloody the faces of the ordinary on every street, the
people going about their dailies, to work, to
school, shopping for the family, their grandfathers
and grandmothers, their uncles, their great-uncles
were there at the grave-side of my flesh, my blood.
With stick, with rock, with snarling dog-catch that
cringing Jewish kid winkled out the neighbor's
basement.

"Don't you know you're supposed to die with the
rest of them-with gun, with gas, with the mighty
blow of my blood lust? Lie down and I will run my
laden cart over your tender bones- rape those girls,
why let it go to waste before we burn them in their
houses."

Shall I repeat the martyrology of Yom Kippur, the
martyrology of every day of Jewish history? Look
on the face of ordinary in the streets without a
tremor because today there is no killing, only the
preparation for killing, only the demonization
anew, only the delegitimization anew, only
preparations anew.

We forget again, the mob only starts with the Jews. The Jews lost six million, but there were fifty million who died before we could turn our face to the ordinary. We try as we might to forget that this was just this time.

We do not forget. We cannot afford to forget, the bodies in our graves cry in our ears, the ash in the air clogs the airways of those yet remaining to breathe.

I am raging, I tear my flesh. I wish to bloody faces of the ordinary in the streets. The bloody times show us nothing has changed in the world. We face it again and again-and the world is blind. The appeasers rule.

I am hungry with the taste, the smell, the craving for revenge for the blood i still see glistening, alive with memory on my body politic.

I am raging, i want to tear flesh, bloody the face of the ordinary, of evil, the bland face of business as usual, when good men do nothing to confront the ordinariness of evil.

Telling Our Stories

Tell stories of the past, meanderings unsought.
Life's dice cast or so we thought.
Family histories from afar impress.
How could we be so cruelly powerless?
Buffeted by forces with intent we could not know.
victims of every hostile wind did blow,
fates determined by every madmen's decree,
lives discarded like flotsam on a storm-tossed sea.
Many vanished without trace
swallowed as in a tidal race,
some few as in a random chance
survived to live and life enhance.
New chapters far across the surf,
planted firmly in new green turf,
live new branches in family blend,
unfolding rich vistas we could not portend.
See new beginnings and new lives in place
bearing fruit, new chances for the human race.
Our numbers grow in every place apace,
learning to feed us all in every crowded space,
searching nature's secrets for prospects bright,
probing in murky futures for a healing light.

Tell our story!

I Call For War

Behold the bitter scenes in the world around me, scenes affecting me only because I be. He sits in comfort, openly proclaiming love for his deity, a deity in whose name he calls for Death, for killing me

I and mine call for peace; offer sacrifice for peace-there is no surcease. In my world my children must with steel encircled be, because he, thousands like he, presidents like he, call for killing.

My God promised that those that bless the people shall themselves but bless-ed be.

My God promised those that curse the people shall themselves but curs-ed be.

God helps he who helps himself.

Why should they who curse me for no reason other than i be sit happily in open rooms, unafraid?

Shall i not do them the service-shall I not send them to the paradise they implore to realize and improve my world?

Where are my sons and daughters to do my bidding?

Shall i not excel in this as i do in many things?

Can my enemy not teach me the single skill in which he excels?

Can i not seek God's perfection and realize His prophecy?

Where are my sons and daughters to do God's bidding?

I call for war!

Ambiguity

Can you live with it?
Can you hold your spit?
You know that to get from here to there apace
you have to cross some barren space.
Our liquid dreams, glowing with internal light,
the ones we cherish, wish to share.
imbued with all our hope's desire, fight
for a life of freedom from immediate care,
we accept some pain to achieve an end to pain,
we accept toil and suffer the vassal's stain.

Study a world of books that does knowledge spark,
amass the credits to meet the lofty needed mark
to earn the job that will pay the wage
to banish fears of the weakness of old age,
to feed our drive for our children's better starting
place,
to overcome the obstacles, goals attain to win the
race.

I rage for those who came before and never had a
chance
to stand where we are standing, mastering the
system's dance.

That time between conception and having the prize
in hand,
doing all the things you must to reach the goal
you've planned,
accepting the dichotomies retained in mind every
living day,
between the miseries of now and what your future
can display.

Doing what you have to do,
swallowing ashes on your tongue,
smiling sweetly to your betters,
hiding the fact that you are strong-
one day master of the foot now upon your neck.
Who's on top at the very end
what count's in life on this whirling speck.

Ambiguity and bearing it is the label that we give
the spaces we sustain in this game of life we live,
spending lives biding time to reach the brightest
goal,
doing what you have to, to sustain steadfast all
your soul,
living through the unending Now to reach your
dreamed of Then,
swallowing-swallow if you can-the inconvenient
question, When?

Attention, Gentlemen!

Do you take alarm, proud rooster, on hearing a
maiden's egg went tweet?
On noise, abroad, some random bawd that you did
prod, for oil money begins to bleat?
These offspring, here, who soon appear, will
someday call their fathers to account.
Little thought spent upon the rent to be paid for the
fun and games of their birthing mount.
Such a simple act, the animal fact that ties us
common with every beast,
we are mere actors in the game, ensuring we
contribute to creation's yeast.

The outcome of this living's dance, the world, long
after us, will duly see.
The custom of creation, there is an unwitting
outcome for conception's spree?
There are billions now abroad, Indians, Chinese,
now a billion or more of the faith of Araby,
each have a story they would impress upon the
lifestyle that our children will in future see.
We, the dwindling few lacking birth dates thought
we their living rules would dictating be,
now begin to realize that numbers which in our
games did little count,

Now define the futures our unthinking mountings
will for our offspring mount.

This is the story of the birds and bees,
this is the story of the flowers and trees.
This is the story we all should know.
Who will tomorrow run the show?

My Time In Your Time

Clickety-clack, the train rolls on, rolls on and on. We are on track! Track time.

Time passing, passing the fixed point, pointing forward and backward, pointing backward are all our memories.

What we are? What have we become? Have we become the What of our memories?

We are stretching back, indeterminately.

The shared memories-we are an amalgam of shared memories from people, books and media-what we saw on YouTube.

How far does our time go back?

Are we not the forward face of past millennia?

Do we not encompass in our minds, in our blood and brains, the memories of the first amphibians struggling forth from a surging sea?

Shall I tell you how it feels to breathe through gills?

Shall i tell you how i howled at the moon, in hunger, frustration and pain from the mouth of my cave?

How did it feel when my skin crackled and burned in flames, birthed in the wrong place, at the wrong time, with the wrong color skin? Or in a tribe different than the one with the torch?

My time is a long time. Will my time end when i end, or shall i be immortal, borne in the flesh and memories-minds touching-of those i leave behind?

Shall my time be your time?

Consequences

Mysteries doggedly dog the fate of every man.
Life yields at its end the consequences of the plan,
written in the sky and on the walls, in people's
lives, subliminal cut and thrust, as the human
strives.

The wages that we earn in actions we gave bare
heed to at the time,
come visiting on silken feet, with slippery treats, to
disrupt the rhyme.
Whether single man or group or industrious nation
state,
actions, unitary or collective, perhaps unknown
and inchoate,
with the fullness of remorseless ever-advancing
time,
assure that the consequences exquisitely fit the
crime.

The hapless victims may never see or relish the
justice that appears,
the traces of their passing, dust and ashes free,
blind shadows, dried-up tears;
somewhere are recorded, annotated, briefly written
on the wind.

The acts themselves create dynamics, silently a
deathhead grinned
at the trail of consequences set in motion,
constructed on a cosmic scale,
to bring ultimate fruition, a foretold conclusion to
this tale.

Those who live them, flushed with power, yet feel
that errant breath of fate,
dismiss the shudder, happily recount them, and
with pride relate
to their companions of their exploits and then go
on to other things,
heedless of what awaits them or offspring, what to
the tribe the future brings.

There is an order in the universe the mind of man
can never plumb,
confronted with its infinities even the brightest are
inevitably struck dumb.
Who can fathom, deconstruct the machinery that
makes it all to run,
conceive the immensity of the spaces we inhabit,
our existences all spun?

Where can we start to view the pattern beyond our
vision, out of sight?
How can we glimpse the many elements we are
blind to in the light?

Advance with care into the life we carelessly,
unconscious, daily spend.
Attend to the actions we sometimes undertake that
we can scarce defend.

We can live our lives in ways that better please the
mind and heart.
aware and sensate of the consequences awaiting us
from the very start.

Midnight Perspectives

I awake to the long shadows thrown by my past-
they stretch behind me. I can read them with a dark
perspective i never see in daylight.The mistakes i
made reach out their long accusing fingers, tracing
the lesions in my mind, their bloody glistenings
sparkle, awakening the pains i do not feel in the
sun's light.

Those long-gone lie out of reach and cannot grant
me the surcease i crave-i must forgive myself.
Those with whom i might dialogue neither know
now nor wait for my midnight aspirations. They
have moved on-as i should- yet i float as a
catatonic in the pool of my regrets-their acid eats at
me. Alone, i must bear my misgivings-my silent
entreaties for a soft review.

I search for my forgiveness, a yearning unrequited.
I vow to lay down my regrets, knowing their long
shadows will greet me when i come this way again.
They are stored with my keepsakes to bedevil the
bright times of my conscious days when my
midnight perspectives, flush with new life, bring
fresh blood to my living life regrets.

What's happening at your house?

Poetical Poetry

The ideas i have dragged from under the cover of my consciousness accumulate in the corners of my mind. I organize them in straight lines, sternly lined up like soldiers at attention, no rhyme permitted.
We have no patience for such affectations. We are too serious. Poetry is too serious. We cannot permit the flightiness of a rhyme.

Wild birds peck. Intestines, glistening, gooey on a plate of leaves, feed the future of the endangered. Shoo! This is not for you! See the Speckled Blue Bunting we favor. Man's horizon brightens! I see tomorrow-my heart, recently bleeding, surges with joy!

Do you share my mystery? Hurrah!

Shall I go on?

Scintillating Rhythm

The tickle of the ivories in a jazzy kind of mood
always tickled my fancy. I could dream i was in a
smoky bar, maybe with a fat cigar in my face-
I don't smoke anymore, not since my daughter got
down on her knees in the middle of the street and
begged me to quit-that was almost fifty years ago.
I can dream can't i?

Just a small combo in the room, a base and a
drummer and the piano player. Maybe a clarinet! I
love the mournful sound they can make-can you
hear it now?
I am not a musical man-a failure, absolute, on the
violin, no ear, no rhythmic sense-but I sure love the
music, whatever the kind. Now i am in heaven,
shivers running up and down my spine. And back
to "ticklin the ivories". I love that.

I could dream my life away to that music.

Life's The Berries

Every morning I have my porridge for breakfast
prepared by the loving hands of the woman i
dreamt of all my adult life, trapped in my other
obligations.

Warm porridge, big flakes of oats the way i like
them. the bowl is chock full of berries,
strawberries, blueberries, loganberries, raspberries-
chock-full.

I glory in them, mashed, mixed and whole-i gobble
them up. I remember when i was young they were
only to look at, not to eat-too precious to eat-too
valuable for the likes of us.

I remember selling them once on the street with my
Dad, shaking the little baskets up and down so they
would look fuller. Sometimes one fell on the
ground. I would snap it up, devour it! That was all
that i could have.

Now i eat my fill.

 Life is the berries!

On Reading My Poetry

It's just the greatest thing
when it's my own song I sing,
knowing better what I think I mean,
better than any other one I've seen.
The things that hurt I'll let you know,
things I'm proud of-hear me crow!
Hear my voice shake with my rage,
that way since I reached my knowing age.
See evil! My voice give wings to my words,
trapped silent without vocal cords!
This is one of writings' joys,
to shout out your words as not mere noise.

What better way to give my message strength
than to expound in person and at length
about the issues lending weight
to the particulars inscribed upon my slate
that shudder me through sleepless nights,
with inward visions that arouse my frights,
or send me dreaming of the better ways
 people might live together better days.

Face the audience you address,
expose yourself and there confess
the inner workings of your mind,

expose responses there in kind.
Face the consequences of what you say
exposed here in the light of day,
know better where you really stay,
examining all the shades of gray,
poring over the detritus, living's rind,
where you are, that you now find
is the place you'd rather be, more or less,
receipt of pain and curse or heaven bless.

Come on in. Welcome, you happy crowd,
as i begin to read my thoughts out loud!

Let Me Tell You!

It is strange to realize, as we stand here in time,
that we once believed these times were good. We
cling to each other, rejoicing in the warmth of
family blood to shield us from the chill of
unknowns, crowding clouds of phantoms round our
shoulders. We hunch them; imagine they are tented
to keep out the visions whirling in our minds.The
acid of fear eats away at our resolve to be brave.

I can tell you it will all be fine, the imagined
shadows will be swept away by bright mornings
bringing new ways of thinking. I can tell you that
better natures will triumph and we will be safe
behind the latching door newly furnished with
bright brassworks. I can tell you i have answers to
all your questions-plans all made to change our
space to better places, new climates and weathers
where the clouds are fluff.

I can tell you all the things i no longer believe.

Death Creeps In

Death slips in, a wraith unseen, the closed door
beneath,
sweet, like summer breezes, bearing yet a wreath.
We have lost an important errant thought
that we have oft with conscious focus sought,
repeated time and time with time to spare,
that we believed we had to share.
Too soon it becomes a habit, then a brake.
Sudden there's a fierce burn and sudden shake,
a sudden lake squall makes the heart quake,
we face the specter now constant here,
threatening lives that we hold near.

Rant and rave at remorseless fate,
offer sacrifices, surrenders, to negotiate
changes in fortunes' cruel decree,
leaving loved ones in full health and free.

Life is a mystery! What has come before? How
come we to this silent shore?
Where do we all go, finished with our work and
closing up the store?
Do we earn ourselves some Brownie stakes?
that we carry over lives to cover our mistakes?
Can a man atone, if he really strives?

for the damage he does to other lives?

Can loving someone with all your soul be a way to
cancel death?
Does a love that does unite you survive after your
last breath?

We cannot separate the ending part from what has
come before,
Death is just another chapter in the story of
living life galore.

A Visit With The French

Can I write a verse here with a lot in it perverse
to criticize unfairly, in concept and rhyming terse,
with words and thoughts that we carefully select
without the merest implication of the politically
correct?
We might express the derogatory about the
splendid British,
or express some ideas inflammatory concerning the
skittish Yiddish,
but in this verse we aim our barbs without mercy at
the French,
expend our humor critically, lay it clearly on the
bench.
Bear with us, we pray, as restraint flies clearly to
the winds
and we dispense our venom, long hidden behind
carefully subtle hints.

We find it hard to take it being from somewhere
else-it really is a wrench-
to be a lower order creature when visiting among
the French,
bred in bone it seems, no matter how you spend
your dreams, whatever the subject, whatever the
cause,

the French knowing best what deserves our full
applause,
forgetting t'was America removed the German
claws,
the French folding away like cards when the issue
seemingly see-saws.

The Italians have flair; the Spanish have their
bulls;
the Portuguese work hard, visiting many foreign
shores,
the Dutch have their dikes, making much of their
new land,
the French have their pride to constantly expand.

They are great for riots in the street,
they love a strike to tie up things so neat,
they paint, there's fashion, and they have sublime
Provence,
they love their dogs upon their knees, esconced.
children are kept hidden in their place,
or not there at all,
they much preferring empty space.
For bread and sauces you know they're known
quite well,
but try to get something urgent done and you really
are in hell.
We know they're really sexy, oft a mistress on the
side,

they're not so good at making kids,
French numbers are on the slide.
They drink a lot of wine; we all love their crisp
baguette,
yet, they stay so nice and thin, serving creamy
sauces we regret.
They worship every inch of ground
that ever has been called French,
but you have to sort a peck of them
to find the one who's a "mensch".

We've now done sufficient damage
to cheerfully mark this Bastille Day,
celebrating our visit here in France.
Think they'll ever invite us back this way?

Awe-ful!

I stand in awe, trembling with joy-
how incomprehensible!
At this instant, for the first time in the history of
the world, the uniquely specific combination,
agglomeration, conglomeration of essences that are
combined in you, have come together to be the
You that you are.

This is happening now for the first and last time in
the history of the world, the galaxy and the
cosmos. Who can count the billions of trillions of
events that have conspire ed to flower this Now-
brought about the Whens, to conceive the Thens to
inspire our happy Nows.

Pinch yourself! Pinch me! Here at this millisecond
the cosmic iterations, interactions, multitudinous
nanocharges that inform atomic bonds,
the seeming-solid spaces we are made of,
making up everything around us,
to feed our illusion of reality in this dimension,
to present us with the existences that we know-
we think we know.
How fortunate we are!
I touch you.
It's awe-ful!

Sparks

The energy that does all living things so animate,
flowing waves, ocean crests we neither see nor
hear, they do resonate in all the fibers of our being,
in all the visions of our seeing.
We are but vessels of some power
that makes our eyes shine in the dark
that regulates the limbs we use,
that fuels the mind with every spark
we show in life, making us peculiarly what we are,
perhaps inherited from a distant star.
There are those on earth that speculate
that the sparks we carry emanate
from the one Prime Mover to which we all equate,
the One who does our entire cosmos dictate.
They say all existence' forces in it do marry
into one entirety, one whole,
one inconceivably gigantic soul
through which our Maker peeks and laughs
as we live our lives and live our gaffes.
Thus we carry a spark, divinity stored carelessly

as an inheritance forever for all our human kin.

If this be so and we have yet free will
to do with our talent either good or ill,
despite the presence of God in us, His very sparks,
we bear the burden of our own life's marks.

Contrary to all the platitudes, we fear
there is evil done in every sphere.
We entreat our Maker, take a stand!
Take these matters well in hand!

It does not seem the world is build-ed so,
constellations roll on with the energy low,
we may carry the spark that God inspires,
but ours is the task to build our own fires.

I Did Not Think

I did not think to be here on the further edge of living.

I did not think to see the blue of the Sorrento Sea rising to meet the black of its dawning sky.

I did not think to see the fire-fly lights of human habitation reaching out to greet the pin-point messages of dying stars.

I did not think to see a reluctant sun's fingering climb of these weathered hills of antiquity.

Millennia of beings built these castling hills of stone, cast down again and again by the earth's convulsions and rebuilt again-they are monuments to life, the tenacity of my kind.

I did not think they would make me feel so small.

I did not think that they would make me feel i should have done so much more.

I am surrounded by the ancient artifacts of giants who came before, the libraries of stored minds on the shoulders, the shouldering shoulders on which we stand to reach higher and higher, standing on our tiptoes, reaching, as we build the edifices of our future times.

Perhaps from here will come the light illuminating the path to freedom from the time limits of our own solar cradle?

Yet, though we are so little a way down that path, I did not think I would be so far along as to be here.

Landing On Earth

I am flying. Not like a bird with my arms flapping, breathing controlled. No, I paid someone to carry me from one place to another. It took a lot of people to do it and they did it.

It would have taken me a long time to walk or drive and i don't know if i would have made it. I am much more fragile these days-i used to think i could do it all-just keep on going

So i flew up in the air and soon, soon, i will land on the earth. I rode my mechanical bird like a fabled prince on a magic carpet dreamt of in another time.

Can you imagine the huffing and puffing of the wind above the feathered carpet of clouds? Looking down they look like the scales on an enormous creature clinging to the spinning ball that is our earth?

It makes me want to hold on to my seat for dear life. We will we have to negotiate that creatured fluff to get back to terra firma-will we see the head of that creature, its claws scrabbling for footing as the ball spins?

I hope to survive this trip. I long to come to terms again with being an earth-bound creature, ant-like, tiny, crawling around on the earth on my fragile feet.

I long to land again on earth.

V

<u>The Latest News</u>

Lifted Up

How marvelous it is that the shape of the crafted
wing lifts up the vessel i am astride! How
marvelous it is that there is a force of nature, if we
but know its secret, which can elevate us to the
skies! Doesn't that mean that we can all be raised
up if only we can learn the secret that will elevate
us?

Our lives are a mystery.
We are living a mystery.
We can all fly like angels
if we learn Nature's secret.
We can, all of us, be lifted up.

Have You Heard?

Have you heard?
We are looking for someone.

We don't know what he looks like.
He could be a she. We all disagree on what he/she
should be, we all disagree on what she/he should
say, but we are all looking because we are all very
unhappy at what we see around us, what we hear
around us, what we have around us and we want it
to change-radically.

We want someone who can make a difference.
We want someone who can rouse our hopes, raise
our hopes from the depths of despair we are in,
someone who can give us a reason to hope,
someone who can change our landscape,
someone who can banish the bad that is here
and awaken the good that is there,
restoring again our faith in ourselves?
We are looking for someone from among us who
can make our better nature the difference.

Have you heard we are looking for you?

Does It Matter?

It is blue, blue, down there where i trawl for
symbols to sustain me.

I look everywhere to find reasons for my being-for
our being.

Should we have a purpose?

The ants clean up after us. Is our purpose to
provide work for ants?

Are we part of Nature's plan to cleanse the world
of the species we eradicate because of our giant
footprint?

Is the pollution of our world a natural process in
the evolution of planets on their way to being
something else?

With the quadrillions of objects and the billions of
suns in our cosmos does it matter?

Listen To the News

When someone trips and falls in Afghanistan
i hear it on a bulletin,
i see it on a tweet,
it's broadcast to my facebook,
soon printed in the daily news,
quickly in a book
so i can read about it on my
Kindle.
My neighbor lost his job.
His unemployment benefits are gone.
His family is on food stamps,
They are regulars at the district food bank.
His son dropped out of college
to take a job at the local gas bar.
His wife left him and took the kids
to go live with her parents.

There was nothing about it in the news.

Cleaning Up The Neighborhood

Read
my mood!
Can i contain
the anger flowing
through me? Can i contain
the rage? Do you read the news?

We
start out
as kids, what
do we know? We go
to school. The big kid pushes
to the head of the line. If we object
he punches us in the face, so we learn to
look away. Or, we form a gang, our own gang.
Of course, he forms a gang too, and they
are tougher than we are because we are
wusses-we don't fight like them at all
because we don't know the dirty
That's how the world really is.
Lots of people have to die
before we are prepared and are
tough enough to do the necessary,
to unite to clean up the neighborhood.

Lines In Sight

Look at the patterns time has printed on your face.
You've earned them, every one.
Remember that grimace when it hurt so bad-it kept
you company quite a while.
Those smile lines, you laughed so hard those times
you thought you'd bust. Admit it, those are worth
having.
Those weeks and months that were so grim, the
pain at the loss of a dear friend, perhaps a lover,
who went on before.

The story of your life is incised there in your flesh,
traced with every passing day, written there in a
language only you understand. Most of us have
forgotten how to read the stories and few of us can
translate.

Can you imagine how those stories have been
written on your very internals?
The inscriptions we see on our faces are
a small sample of libraries that have been inscribed
into the tapestry we bear within. The surge of the
adrenals to power hand and leg, the trickle of the
hormones to fire heart and mind, the rise and fall of
acid to corrode our vital parts, the huff and puff of

pressures to strain the plumbing we all depend upon-all tell the story of our living, hidden out of sight.

The gravity of our situation has worked its magic on all the being we still offer. We bear the weight of the world and it shows in every part.

The lines in sight are not even the half of it.

Enjoy reading the lessons of your life!

The Joke's On Us

Can
you believe
it? We are an
insignificant speck
in the ultra trillions of an
expanding cosmos we struggle
to understand. Of course we are
the central focus of the Maker of all
this Unknowable we inhabit. Naturally!

Can
I contain
the riotous laughter
that coats my cheeks with tears?

The joke's on us.

A Hopeful Note

The sun rose today.
Yesterday's brilliant sunset,
the celebration of day's end,
a convulsion of the color spectrum
that made us ooh and ahh at our witnessing,
has birthed a hot new beginning to our Now.

We are alive.
There is no limit
to what we can do today
if we have but the will.

We remember what we did yesterday.
We have some plans for today.
We retain the potential to change our tomorrows.

Now we can better spend our lives .

.

The Roar of Righteous Anger

Did you see me on your YouTube?
Was my message strong or weak?
Did they broadcast me on Oprah?
Did millions me on twitter seek?
Did they blog me there on Facebook?
Was i a feature on CNBC?
Did they hack my song on your website?
Was my solo heard for free?

Will my mystery go viral?
Will the story i must tell
assail a billion eardrums-
hear the music round me swell!
I am a prophet of the future
sharing the chaotic visions that i see,
rousing silent masses into action
to protect our lives 'neath Freedom's tree.

Let me hear the roar of righteous anger,
as silent sleepers wake
to the dangers confronting us,
the evil forces we must brake.
The existential threat is clear.
Make a fuss,

let fly the news
of the harbingers in our midst.
The phantoms in the mist persist,
understand the portents in our media,
get, of the messages, the gist.

Our teachers have often taught us.
evil in this world triumph will
if men of good will remain silent
as the weakest suffer from the shrill.

Arise now and stand together!
Awake, construct the barricades we must
to protect the freedoms we have builded,
the freedoms we all hold in trust.